Gerard Woodward was born in north London in 1961. He studied painting in London and Falmouth and anthropology at the LSE. In 1989 he won the major E.C. Gregory Award and he was recently awarded an Arts Council Bursary.

AFTER THE DEAFENING

BY THE SAME AUTHOR

Householder

AFTER THE DEAFENING

Gerard Woodward

Chatto & Windus
LONDON

First published in Great Britain in 1994

1 3 5 7 9 10 8 6 4 2

© Gerard Woodward 1994

Gerard Woodward has asserted his right under the
Copyright, Designs and Patents Act, 1988 to be
identified as the author of this work

Acknowledgements are due to the editors of the following publications,
in which some of these poems first appeared:
Poetry Book Society Anthology 1991, *Poetry Book Society Anthology
1992*, *Ambit*, *Rimbaud Centenary 1991*, *Poetry Review*, *Verse*, *Times
Literary Supplement*, *The Rialto*, *Gairfish*, *The Gregory Anthology 1987–
1990*, *Oxford Poetry*, *PN Review*, *Iron Magazine*, *Poetry Durham*

Published in 1994 by
Chatto & Windus Limited
Random House, 20 Vauxhall Bridge Road
London SW1V 2SA

Random House Australia (Pty) Limited
20 Alfred Street, Milsons Point, Sydney
New South Wales 2061, Australia

Random House New Zealand Limited
18 Poland Road, Glenfield
Auckland 10, New Zealand

Random House South Africa (Pty) Limited
PO Box 337, Bergvlei, South Africa

Random House UK Limited Reg. No. 954009

A CIP catalogue record for this book is available from
the British Library

ISBN 0 7011 6271 6

Typeset by SX Composing Ltd, Rayleigh, Essex
Printed in Great Britain by
Mackays of Chatham PLC, Chatham, Kent

Contents

THE BIRDS

You haven't noticed,
But while you've been
Sitting there, nearly

A thousand birds
Have roosted in the playground
Behind you. The roundabouts

And swings are living
And feathery. And now
You remember that constant

Fluttering at the back
Of your mind, the cyclist
You knew about, the rook

That flew in his face
And ruined him.
It makes sense now.

There was a certain
Turbulence up there,
A rumour spreading

Through the rookery. The trees
Were a nightmare
To walk under.

THE PRINCIPLES OF FLIGHT

The astronauts are up
In von Braun's cherry tree
Throwing cherries at his red face.

They boast of their everlasting
Footprints, and the fuss
They kicked up on the Sea of Tranquillity.

Von Braun cries to himself, his
Old, gentle face measled
With these sweet

Little missiles he
No longer flinches from. The nearest
He ever came to the moon

Was when he first met Eva
That night in the Bay of Rainbows.
Christ she was like

A room full of machines, of marine
Engines built by Burmeister
And Wain of Copenhagen,

She was HMS
Cristoforo Colombo inside out.
It was she who severed

His ball and chain of gravity
Teaching him the principles of flight,
Of falling fruit.

And that arrogant
Orchard of Americans were
Welcome to their weatherless world.

2

THE KIDS

At first the adults didn't notice
When a pulley came into motion
And windmills made of paper
Cups turned as a cupful of sand
Descended. Later a nail suspended
On a length of cotton twisted
So the torque of thread, when released,
Sent it dizzying round like mad
Until the marble was triggered,
Tumbling down chutes, shafts
And staircases of balsa wood
To trigger something else, never
Reaching a real conclusion
Or purpose other than movement finishing.

They realised the rocking horse
Had failed or fallen when Charlene
Gripped her pink hammer and called
'Sue, Sue, give me the nail'.
Lego, Meccano, the dolls' house
Becoming a mansion, the train-set
Doubling its radius every other day,
The nursery couldn't contain them
So they'd moved to the garden and begun
To build. Blueprints were drawn
In non-toxic crayons. Architects
Asserted themselves and spires appeared
From which jacks told any time at all.
And no one noticed even when the house
Fell into shadow and the kids
Were climbing gantries to build higher,
Except the patio nicotiana closed
Its petals, and someone in the house
Turned up the brightness on the *Six O'Clock News*.

A blue and yellow crane moved on wheels
With silly faces up a spiral track
That coned impossibly up,
And the kids gathered at the viewing
Platform and looked down on the real house
With its tiny rooms and the people who spoke
And cried and ate like real people,
Who were coming out now and looking up.
'Not yet,' the kids said, winding up
A final piece of clockwork. 'Not yet.'

LITTLE PTOLEMY

Little Ptolemy,
He tore the fundamental
Pages from my thrillers

And drew the moons he'd
Seen through his homespun
Telescope in sawdust,

Predicting eclipses, transits.
He messed all my clocks up
But was kind to my peacocks

Even when they drew blood.
He lit his Monte Cristos
At our hot forge

And brought my Morris
Back from the dead
When he yanked the

Digitalis out of her
Tank and filled
The hollowness with fuel.

His rambling roses
Caught my hair. He
Had a song for everything

But thought in Latin, spoke
In equations, L
Equals M over P

Squared meant something
Like I love you, Mummy.
I loved him, Little

Ptolemy, explaining
And repairing like he did.
I no longer had the shakes, although

Stranded in my Agatha
Christies, I'm glad I had him,
That I should have such clever blood.

THE EXPLORER'S SON

The weathermen said, 'Be brave'.
He had no choice, luscious

Though the North Pole was,
All that unveined marble

Like the ruins of Michelangelo's
Studio. If he wanted

The iceberg he should
Have had it, hollowed it,

Floated south on his knees
And into the record books,

Until his cold church
Thawed off Nova Scotia.

It didn't happen like that.
First, he lost confidence

In his teeth. They hurt
On lollies, were dirty. His grin

Was buried in the minds
Of everyone he liked. He who'd

Encouraged his Dad to stand up
For himself, like the man

Who in a deep drift tethered
His mare to the top of the steeple,

Couldn't even sever himself
From the body of the continent,

The main shelf. Next, he suffered
A longing to clean windows

And thought that everywhere
There were reflective buildings

Full of workers, but all
He could see was the passage

Of clouds, and through rose-tinted
Spectacles what was otherwise

Tragedy, the polar wastes blushing
Like countries of nothing

But sunset. Gifted, he could see
Through everything, therefore

Nothing. Then he thought about
His own memorial, of how

Applause would be followed
By bouquets tossed on the ice

Where they shattered,
That he couldn't pick up,

Because he was inside
Looking out through thick windows

And seeing someone compiling
Signatures so that this would never

Happen to children again.
Would never be commonplace.

MILK OFFENSIVE

One night I dreamt the enemy
Bombers passed over the usual
Targets and bombed instead
The fields of cows.

And the ministers took
All the surviving mothers' milk
To save in a frozen underground
Complex the size of Coventry.

And I was walking through
These boulevards of sweet ice
And thinking of how one day all
Would thaw and flow and flood,

And at the armistice
We would drink our fresh
Breakfasts again, and the bones
And teeth of our children grow.

THE BANKRUPT'S WEDDING

The seething bakers tore down the whole cake.
Leaving a rubble of currants and columns they filled
Their sleeves with good luck and left.

Was it so unreasonable, when the cycle
Of debt had passed right through the creditors
And come back to the father,

That when the florists came they hissed
At his daughter and snatched their unpaid-for
Blooms back, that spirit merchants

Should rattle their wines back to their bottles,
Or silkworms drag themselves up the aisle
And sip at the long, milky dress of the bride?

EVENING MEAL

Good food became better.
The brides-to-be
Fell asleep while making
Their beds. They had
To be dragged from their quilts.

We made inroads
Into a bottle of Fleurie
And remembered vineyards
We didn't know,

And a bounding,
Orange, prizewinning retriever
Who seemed to know
The cup was his.

And then our plates were empty,
And neither of us could recall
Having swallowed, but felt
Instead different landscapes
And varieties of livestock.

A church opened
And brides came in their silk.
And neither of us could say
Why this was wrong, or if it was,
Except that our room had changed
Somehow, as if we'd had visitors.

A NOCTURNAL BREAKFAST

The match has shown
A breakfast in this room.
The hours are wrong.

Before, it was just Earl Grey
Coming out of the dark,
But now it is confirmed,

A breakfast in the middle
Of the night. Its eggs
Give shadows big

As men.
Cereals quake in their milk.
Crumpled bacon

Cools on porcelain.
I had my suspicions, hearing
The little percussion

Of it being set.
Forks await the comfort
Of my hands.

I think this may be
The last ever breakfast.
Hens died laying these

Ultimate eggs.
Cows drained themselves
Of their last few saucerfuls,

Lay down in blue grass
And yawned
a pink yawn.

This slice of toast
Contain's America's
Final field of wheat.

The salt-cellar
Holds the white
Residue of Cheshire.

Seeing plates I think
How St Austell's hills
Will nevermore

Bring forth crockery.
I cry salt over the egg
Of my nocturnal breakfast.

The match says it all
In failing. No one will see
That marmalade again.

A COOK'S WARNING

A kitchen's not for thinking in.
It doesn't mix with pans
Lip-full of boiling water,
Or a dozen onions needing
Peeling and pickling.

That's why it's so full of rules,
Like don't let a loop
Of kettle flex hang from the edge
Of the fridge, or a child
Near boiled jam before it cools.

And it's so easy to forget,
If lovesick, say, how in there
The commonplace can suddenly
Be red hot, or carry enough
Charge to shock an infant dead.

So peeling and pining
Should be kept apart
Or the knife might lose
Its composure, and cut
Through what doesn't need slicing.

It could all end in tears
If the tinned steamed pudding
Goes off like a bomb, fills
Your eyes with sultanas and leaves
A ceiling stain that lasts for fifteen years.

It happened to my mum.
So be collected in a kitchen.
Follow recipes and safety procedures
To the letter. Remember, it's your
Home's most dangerous room.

IN THE CRIMSON KITCHEN

Fishing, you hooked a John Dory.
We cooked it en croute
With mozzarella and sun-dried
Tomatoes. A sprig of marjoram.
What a catch to land
In your own house! But it was
The colour, crimson lake,
You fished in, and we'd painted
The whole kitchen with it.

We tried to identify the cause
Of the progress of red in our lives,
What stirred in the eight
Living rooms of our hearts
When we took this course. I wanted
To become Governor of Jersey
And conquer and seed
The world with tomatoes.

You wrote a paint catalogue,
Naming each emulsion Strawberry
Fields, and so incarnadined
Everyone's interior. Our doctor
Poked into our red dreams
And pulled out a roasted cherry,
Saying it was our tiny heart.
We waited for bad weather
And then locked him out.

Before, when that woman tried to part
Frozen burgers with our best knife,
She nailed herself to her food.
It wasn't right, our chopping-board
Stained with lives and liver.
People were afraid of our kitchen.
Now, once a month, you dress
Yourself in red from top to toe
And lose yourself in there.
And I witness the levitation
Of pans that fill themselves,

And when the dinner's ready
A piece of the kitchen walks
And serves it. Beetroot
Becomes you. We make Russian
Soup and drink it from a grail.
With red cabbage we serve up
Scarlet salads. This rose
Has made us madder.

I believe, until we welcomed
This colour and saw it as
The primary of primaries, the very
Ketchup of life, we had worried
So much about what could go wrong
In a kitchen. But mistakes
Don't show up now. It was the best
Way. The only way, in fact.

AFTER THE DEAFENING

You write me letters
Even though I'm still with you.
Our ears, clumsy

Treble clefs, just overwrought
Ornaments of flesh, now,
Since those local disasters.

And all our surviving neighbours
Share this visible world
Where men drive nails

Home with kisses, missing
The birds' traffic of whereabouts,
Their melodious debate

On the ownership of trees.
Even history's rendered harmless,
Its wars just airy turbulence;

Krakatoa's red mime,
Nagasaki's dazzling silence
That leaves its ring of deaf,

Like us, these are things
To fall asleep to, the shifting
Of midnight husbands,

The world making itself comfortable.
Our screams come out as
Nothing more than an arm's length of breath

That doesn't even wake us.
Even though you are next to me
I write you letters.

ORANGES

Another night I dreamt I was
A citizen of Seville
And keeper of the orchard
That fed England with marmalade.

I woke, and everything was orange
And oranges. Not just the dog
But my wife exhibited
Her ten fingers like coarse-cut

Golden Shred that made me
Rush to the supermarket
And promenade among the preserves,
And when I left I found myself

In countryside where any lane
Would lead me deeper
And deeper into orange
And orangeness, and, yes,

I was picking citrus fruits
In Kent, and drew my
Thumbnail across one's skin
And released a mist of acid

That soaked us both.
And she said, 'Don't worry,
It's just autumn. It happens
Every year.' 'But not like this,'

I said, although I wasn't worried,
It was just that I'd planned
To manufacture marmalade
Here, to be a sweet magnate,

To spread it thickly
Over England, to conserve
The whole of it, to shine
On the tip of every knife, every breakfast.

FLORITE

If coal is the oppression
Of the forest, then this,
Darling, that I've cut
For our wedding ring,
That burns yellow where
It should, on your marriage
Finger, is the oppression
Of Gardens. Found beneath
The coal measures
It is the petrification
Of untold daisies, marigolds,
Violets and primaeval lupins,
Because in those days
Before trees, everyone
Studied at the College
Of Flower Arrangers
And then forgot their
Lessons, and an empire
Was built on floral clocks
Spelling everybody's name,
And Mother's Days grew
Into a geological era,
Closing the book
On the very first garden
And keeping it between
Thick pages of rock
Laid down before
And after. And now
If our anniversaries
Get out of hand, and we
Exchange bouquets
Made from entire gardens,
If our celebration overtakes
Its reason and drowns us
And our city in chrysanthemums,

I will look at this tiny
Garden centre rounding
Your finger and see
The nurseries there,
Trays and trays
Of seedlings nearly ready.

ILLUMINATIONS

In Blackpool, once, a fish
And chip vendor switched
The vinegar in his little
Blackpool Towers for red
Wine. A man blind from birth
Seasoned his cod and saw

Blackpool and boo-hooed
At so much: politicians
High-kicking on the South Shore
Like the very first amphibians,
Children looping the loop,

With the sea a restless
Edge of everywhere,
And his tears fell like December
And he became a great
Distance from himself
When they landed on the carpet
Of the Winter Gardens where
A man held two tablets
Of glass, his transparent
Decalogue, and read
Their vitreous text,
His head moving from one
To the other, as if noting
The passing of multitudes.

It was the movement
That got him. Everything moved.
And outside a politician
Cartwheeled past, this
Black hub and spokes
Of a man rolling, delighted,
Like a minister of transport.

THE KNOWLEDGE

He knew what fillings
Hid in sandwiches postmen
Ate in Postman's Park.
He could taste their meat pastes
And could taste the postmen's
Tongues that tasted.

From his bed he heard
The howl of dogs,
Could see which breeds mated in fields in
Castelnau, Seven Kings and Child's Hill,
Could say sit and feel
That London's every bitch obeyed.

History was his. He heard the gurgle
Of lost rivers: Fleet, Tyburn. The Thames
Was his river of love, and sewers
Flowed in a similar vein. Those streams
Will burst through roads
And flow again, he thought.

One night he dreamt
Of all the flowers that came
After the Great Fire,
Making meadows out of those
Charred acres. And the bees
That crackled from Temple to Cripplegate.

The vanished prisons: Coldbath,
Millbank, Clink. He grinned
As Bedlam became the War
Museum. People bolted into
Bed. All his night-time reading
Was the A to Z, and all his childhood reading too.

It's index
Was fixed, somehow,
In his mind, its columns
Of names like the stolen
Pylons of Euston. Useless arches,
He sometimes feared, that propped nothing.

Still. He thought. He knew
It all before the Aldwych, and when
The Strand was really that.
He had like Wren the whole thing
Held. Londoner. He thought.
And it all came into his head.

YOUR SHELL-LIKES

Listen. I thought
I tipped your head and red
Wine poured from them.
I filled the glass. Alas.
Listen. Didn't we think
All flesh came from that
Field Michael Jones's father
Ploughed and doesn't anymore,
That we are the increments
Of a thousand autumns piled
Up like unread books?
But the bakeries take their
Tythes of wheat, and bread
Is the proper outcome of soil,
And we are the proper end of bread
Which makes these exaggerations
Of yours, either side of your head,
Most puzzling, unnecessary flesh.
Yes. Listen. In front of the sun
They glow red like two
Miniatures of spirit. More wine.
I will not let them burn and if
Those folds catch extra music
Let me eavesdrop. Those things
You hear me with. They are
The unlit corridors I will walk
Down one day shouting. Or I
Will preserve them as mementoes
That day, painted a cheerful
Colour and pinned to the wall.

Otherwise just listen. A gardener
Would have taken a millennium
To reach such flowers. Are they
The lilies we must find in bread shops,
With the thinking part still
There but somehow somewhere else,
Something like a question mark?
Listen. Bend them. Oi!

THE SCENE OF THE CRIME

If only he'd known then
How he was history in the making,

Was out of the ordinary,
Even though his evening

Had been like all his others,
Except for one detail.

When they came they seemed
Really to care, labelling each

Fragment of his given vase,
And matching the flowers

With it, fantastic! Picking his
True hairs from soft

Furnishings, anything
To put their fingers on. Historians

Of a few minutes, they researched
With painful scholarship

A moment in his life
He barely remembered, saw steps

Taken in a measure
Of spotless lino, his now

Registered trade mark
Of skin on the least thing,

Even the lemon zester. They even
Fostered his generations

Unborn when they froze
The teeny gem of semen

They found a long way from
The bed or bathroom.

And this place wasn't even his.
They must have loved him.

STRONG MAN

There is only so much
A man can take. So he
Packed his weights
And went. Dwarfs wept.

They didn't mean it,
Ludicrous though he looked
In his leopard-skin
And waxed moustache,

But they couldn't talk.
The woman who every night
Managed to find the gorilla
In herself has lost it

Since he left. The lion
Tamer treats his thousands
Of scratches, The Flying
Tyrells their bruises,

And the bearded lady
Has rediscovered her
Philishave. One night
She thought she saw the vast

Butterfly of his shoulder-blades
Take wing as he hoisted
Another ton, or bent a girder
On his baby-smooth head,

And they wished they could
Untell all those jokes
About biceps like cooking-apples,
Grizzlies, or the fear

Of shaking hands with a mountain.
Instead the midgets practise
Stilts and totter round the tilting
Mass of his vacant caravan.

THE SHRINKAGE

Trying to stand up
For Bonapartes,

Instead he undid
All he'd done, visited

Places he'd hoped he'd
Seen the last of, like childhood,

All heroes, and saw
The wife ripen like redwood

To an impossible mother
Staying late with a man

From work, not ironing,
Even in hope. He whispered

His rage in the high
Church of her ear, and found

Himself the pet of pets,
And then the pests

At eye level set
Their agendas.

Next dust, the one
Thing he could fit,

The endless demolition
It meant, or hair like a virgin

Forest plundered and sent
Downstream from another country

Where she sat at her mirror,
Singing and combing.

OXFORDSHIRE

The men are saying the rock
Required for the new motorways
Will leave a hole the size
Of Oxfordshire three feet deep,

Which is another way of saying
A hole the size of England
One inch deep. But Oxfordshire
Will do. And then I saw that quarry

And all the roads leading
Into Oxfordshire ending
At a Beachy Head three feet deep,
And the spires ground to gravel

And spread over hard shoulders,
And the rivers robbed of their flow
And all the birds dumbstruck
And picking over the aggregates

Hopelessly. But elsewhere, roads,
Broad and smooth, like endless
Volcanic beaches, and Oxfordshire
Stretched like elastic

Across the breadth of all other
Counties, flowing with vehicles,
As if the river of life
Had thickened somehow, to mud or honey.

SLEEPING PARTNERS

It is true to say the world
Is always two hemispheres,
One light, the other dark,
And in the dark half they sleep.

I phoned London Transport
And told them of a bus conductress
I knew who snoozed the whole
Route from Muswell Hill

To Edmonton, missing all her fares.
Zzzzzzzzzz was all I heard
Down the phone. The Noise Abatement
Society was holding a demonstration

In Victoria Street, each
Placard saying simply, 'Shhhh',
And a rank of kids at the front
Held each of the letters of the word

SILENCE. I took the train home
And sat amongst the commuters, all
Of whom had nodded off by Abbey Wood.
Dark now, they slept

Like half the world, with me
The only one awake in a crowded
Carriage. A secretary in a nylon blouse
I didn't know from Eve

Leant her head on my shoulder
And dribbled into my breast pocket.
I have her pocketful of spit now,
It makes my pencils draw nothing.

It was their faces. All the same,
Equalized by dozing, undriven
By the need to muscle up
An invoiced slogan,

They approached babyhood
Further down the line, a notion
Of babyhood that stopped me
Bellowing 'Wakey! Wakey!'

When the stations came. I didn't
Need to. What defied explanation
Was how each woke before
His or her stop, and they left,

Emptying the carriage
Until it was just me
And the salivating secretary
Moving peacefully towards

The Kent coast. And I
Wondered if she would wake
In time, or, indeed, if I
Could dare to fall asleep

In partnership, and if we could
Slumber so deeply we would
Both miss our stations, and pass on
To beaches, oysters, grottoes.

SOMETHING ELSE

Her hair dyed auburn,
A hook she cut

From herself and kept,
As if its riddance

Might take something else
With it, or she

Could picture from it
How she was at the moment

Of severance; troubled,
Determined. The mirror

Useless, and in it
The failure of seeing

Herself.
Counting

The gardens home
From London Bridge,

I am thinking how a city
Like this is eighty per cent

Grass, where one lawn
Seems to cause the next,

As if a road of meadows
Was building itself

Before me, leading
To a city that doesn't

Look like ours,
Whose museum

Holds a single hair
From the beard of a prophet,

And how from this, for some,
The whole face flowers.

AN ADDRESS TO THE BARBER

Is it our failings
You have been seen
To hold to your naked
Chest after hours,

Or scoop up in that
Sack of yours, for what?
To fill the embroidered
Pillows of a cottage industry?

Ellen's sure her postman's
Pony-tail brushed her cheek
One night, and he's
Another customer of yours.

At school your son is said
To have boasted of the largest
Guy Fawkes on Fleece Hill. Is this
Effigy filled with us? Have you

Reconstructed those who trust
You with their throats and ears
To turn your little one's Bonfire
Night green and weak?

We cannot tolerate this
Disrespect for what is after
All part and parcel of ourselves
And suggest that future trims

Should come with special bags
In which to store our chaff
And take home to do with
What we will.

ROOM

A thousand years.
It makes things seem
So slight. If an

Archaeologist brushed
Gently its grit
Of eras off, or if

Someone discovered
In it signs
Of new animals, we would

Say this room that was
Lived in one thousand
Years is something retrieved.

The stairs that led
There, a zigzag
In the memory,

The place itself, only
Ever crowded, and
Everyone eavesdroppers,

Everyone saying 'I
Like it here,' and knowing
It. Perhaps the lively

Spirit of a slot
Meter still counting
Kilowatt hours,

Or above the fireplace
A weak tree of soot,
Coal's forest regained.

A place where stone
Might weigh nothing, but
Split seconds tons.

YARN

When that catch slipped
Onto deck the crew
Stepped back and cried
Seven seas down their faces.

The Medusa soaked
In her Pacific. Her little
Forest of oaks remembered
Treehood. What thing,

Fed on grit and sunk plunder,
Feeling the grain of the deck
With uncoloured limbs, they thought,
Was this? And wished it back

In hot fathoms beneath sound.
And each thought of sonatas,
A pianist's fingers dripping,
And applause like tethered birds.

A SAILOR'S THOUGHTS ON DRY LAND

I
The Lighthouse. A building
That walks on water. Or all
That's left of an older

Venice. Where candle-power
Lives and looks out
Of its window all night.

The ambition of all
Houses whose lofts might
Otherwise be brilliant.

II
How Able's Rock needed one
Then, when Methane Princess
Gashed her hull and tilted

Down, her decks ocean's
Playground as her crew
Found a lifeboat and then

An island where they counted
Up on white hands hands
Lost. Nameless land,

Passed over by the builders
Of empires, it didn't
Even have a house

But for this,
Their vessel upturned
On the one pink beach.

III
They soon noticed the likeness
Of ship and roof timbers,
A clinker-built hull now roof-beams

Of any manner of roof,
Tie-beam, king-post,
Double hammer-beam,

Which made them, especially
The navigator, whose brazen
Dividers strode charted waters

With arms akimbo, think
Of first and last houses,
Of the hotel on the cliff

Whose real master
Bedroom was the cave
In the cliff below ground floor.

IV
The buildings that have survived.
In praise of architecture
A bomb was devised that left

People in ruins, not buildings.
They wept at the true value
Of property, and in the little

Church with a replica
Of a ship in it they lifted
A mat and found

A surprisingly yellow
Brass, and didn't
Know if this was history

Ancient or modern, or if
It meant that the end of all
Endeavour was butter.

V
And he held Daisy's
Rancid hand, that he would soon
Eat, but saw her instead

As a tower higher
Than Sears, in whose crimson
Elevators he travelled to the huge

Vents of central heating from which steam,
A building-full, a crisis of evaporation,
The perpetual vanishing that he wanted

To cease, seceded.
As if buildings were homes
To unthought ideas that bloomed

As thought-bubbles yet to be filled.
But they honeymooned at the Cliff Hotel
And he sang 'Daisy, sing me your song

While you've still a mouth
To sing it.' It was the one
Place he hadn't kissed,

And the hotel slipped, room
By room, into the sea.
'If you can drown on dry land

then what's the point
Of Atlantic?' he said as their matrimonial
Four-poster voyaged.

VI
He thought of Rievaulx
Rebuilding itself,
Or Eiffel, up there, Spiderman

In a topper, striding
The girders with a spanner,
Unscrewing his massive achievement.

HORSE LATITUDES

They come to me, dripping,
To this day, in Nantucket,
Bombay, Darwin, the horses

Whose ungainly dives
I supervised for the sake
Of the thirsts of thirty-nine

Hands slaked in a ship
Whose skipper boasted of his oaks
And corks, the woodlands

Fashioned by shipwrights
Into ship, inflating the price
Of wood and so driving

Men underground for coal,
Starting the internal
Combustion engine which dragged

The black water from the mines
And ended the need
For animal traction.

*

The horses
In the unsteady hold
Were just coughs and flashes,

An avenue of safe flesh,
Useful musculature,
Fit to take the weight

Of revolutions of politics
And industry. I would
Rather have died

Of thirst in driest desert
Than goad those thoroughbreds
To their surprise deaths.

Our funds of water
Should have taken doldrums
Into account, we should

Have had enough to let
A warship drink through all
Its fiery campaign, our horses

Should have gulped wine
From golden pails. But to drown
Our own living cargo,

To go down in books
For a flotsam of ruined and soaking
Carcasses beached on some delta!

*

Hippocampus, Grizzle, Black Agnes,
Carman, Marengo, Savoy,
Europe's surplus, if you

Had seen it, that riderless,
Floundering cavalry, a game
Of chess, all knights,

Played between continents. And later,
When the winds picked up
And we made the Cape with just

Our alcohol, in those
Vacant stables just a sweetness
Of air to tell you the world

Had once had horses.
Now the sea was back to itself
I loathed its absence of pasture,

Nor could I steer by Pegasus again,
And to this day have never
Put my heart in machines.

DOROTHY'S LOVER

Standing for a year in a cornfield,
Menaced by dew, it brought out
The worst in me. I saw then

Where it might end, and developed
A rational fear of magnets
But wiped miles of iron oxide

Cassette tape, ran like mad
From the rain, shunned the oceans
I kept seeing. Didn't dare weep. We all

Have a right to be frightened of something.
But she did me a world of good.
There's nothing like love, I've always

Said it. At first I thought
She might given under my
Sheer weight, but how she

Soothed me with the multigrade
Of her love, honed me on some
Lathe-like fidelity that let her

Even embrace the tangle of my swarf,
Her arms carved with red crescents,
But that was us through and through.

Our lovemaking, she said, was like
Sitting on a knife-edge,
And it took me right back

To the smith and his lovely anvil,
And I feel like I've come to the meltdown
And will be money any minute.

Or she works with her oxy-acetylene
And she can craft what she likes,
I love it, scrapped, processed, reminted.

THE OTHER HAND

You thought, being November, anything
You touched would be enriched.

How can you account for the forest?
Someone has made a killing there.

Or that your girlfriend will never
Feel the sub-light of buttercups

Confirming her desires? The children
Need their buoyant, golden milk.

All you have given them is what
They already know; white

And tasteless. Your invalid
Mother thought of the treasures

You brought her for breakfast,
But now finds just brown bread

And brown eggs. And what doesn't
Glow anymore at the tip of a cigarette,

In the grate or heart, was frozen
By you. The pilot lights have

Withdrawn into their clay. Marriages
Wrecked. Bonds have melted

And dripped slowly and unseen
From fourth fingers. Ears and necks

Denuded. Daylight has lost
Its certainty. These are just some examples.

Tarantulas are now a real
Possibility in every fruit store.

TRAITOR

The Continent of Boys had been scrapped,
He told us, the day the playgrounds

Were silenced. And plans
For nothing but horse chestnut and floodlit

Cricket in every city reduced
To one tiny infant dependency

On the edge of Empire he hoped
To govern one day. Everything

Happened at once, he said. First,
His pets refused their food

And starved. Mary, on her
Last legs, limped into the garden

To show him the graves of all
The birds and mice she'd killed,

For the sake of some sort of atonement,
He thought, but built a pet

Cemetery anyway, and there were
Rows of crosses made of twigs bound

With blades of grass for ever,
It seemed. Then he found

He was the origin of a colourful plague
That passed right through classes

Five, Six and Seven, (Miss Yeoman's).
Boys and girls were suddenly

Too old to be his friends. And just when
He thought he'd learnt the language,

It changed. One girl refused
Him her orange, even though

He'd seen it before, vivid in front
Of her purple pullover. Those colours

Stayed with him. But he no longer
Compared lunches. He turned delinquent

And one night stripped the vicar's
Fruit trees with a fishing net, landing

A catch of dark, ripe fruit, and truanted,
First from school, and then everything.

And now he's here, getting used
To new faces on the currency. We

Love him. We always have.
We always will. He tells us of

His fondness for his memories
Of the Forty-Five Landslide, the White

Heat of Technology Speech that made
Him want to carve mile-high

Statues of ordinary people. He
Remembers his Grandmother, and how

She is still her own woman. But then
Again, he remembers the Three

Bears, and how in his country,
Last year, seventy-four people

Were murdered before they'd
Reached the age of one.

BLACK COMEDY

We were in stitches
And savage with it.
Joy's face became
Her father's, and her father's

Sunburnt and how
He howled, and
The granddaughter grew ancient,
Her nose a peach stone

Like her grandmother's.
Other faces undressed,
Lips were hitched
Like skirts and never-before

Seen gums shone like
The hard edge of nakedness.
Felicity's face flowered
Like open-heart surgery

With her tongue the giveaway
That made me want
To take a surgeon's
Thread to mend those rents

Or at the very least
Whisper 'Pull yourself
Together.' But I couldn't
Speak through my own

Noise. I had never seen
The Chinaman in my brother
Before, his eyes folded
Like that. As if Mum's

Death had made us all
Foreigners, and the funeral
Had been a sketch that had us
Killing ourselves. It was funny.

DOMESTOS

It was the provost of the Royal
College of Sanitary Engineering

Who gave the lecture that year.
He drew his drains. He spoke

For a while on how
The West End's sewers

Were becoming clogged with
Restaurant fat, in which

He saw a pretty analogy
With heart disease in middle-

Aged men, which made him think
Of the German sculptor

Who'd made a statue out of
Human fat called 'Liberty

Sheds Light on Some
Political Conundrums', which in turn

Led him on to a discussion
On the morality of bleach

Which, he said, like Rapunzel's
Tears, has a purifying effect,

Though won't restore sight. Indeed,
If liquids had a political

Leaning then bleach would be
A fascist through and through,

Its users were discriminators
In nature, who thought the natural

World merely an idea
Repeating itself *ad nauseam*,

Who despised the very idea
Of what he called the *Gesellschaft*

Of dirt, the association
Of germs who would

In this commonwealth
Live as in the Golden Age

When everyone was everyone
Else's banquet. Bleach, he said,

Is the Devil's own vintage
And concluded with a sad tale

Of a parlour maid who drank some.
A vote of thanks was given

And the provost acknowledged our applause
By raising a glass of Château Latour.

THE HOUSE CROESUS BUILT

Would you really
Want to live in this
Ingot, when all

Who leave leave richer?
Touch it and your
Fingers are small fortunes.

Yes, its roof holds off
Rainy days, but for how much
Longer, when the plumber cuts

Out good pipes
And guests hawk
Light bulbs through jewellers,

Or even pinch cobwebs
To give as gifts from this
Bright and famous house?

In a month the stairs have worn
To what it takes a church
Four hundred years,

And vague footprints
Lead everywhere. No bank
To deposit this,

It is its own soft fort
And who can steal a building?
Enough unknowing burglars

Can. The friction of visitors
Means it's thinning fast,
And when the walls start

To buckle, and the last glare
Of dust is carried off on soles,
Will the secret bullion

Of its foundations really
Give the worms their luggage,
So they drag down its riches, millionaires?

DREAM COTTAGE GAME

I've won a cottage.
I can't believe it. I matched
The lips of famous people
With their eyes and now
I've hit the jackpot. The cottage
Of my dreams. I'm scared.

I'm not sure if I want this prize,
Even though it's the luckiest
I've ever been. I'm on a winning
Streak, keep finding money,
And this morning caught the train
That left five minutes before
The one that crashed. Every time
I think about the telephone
It rings. There it goes again. Hold on.

IVY MOTHS

I
Dad nearly dead,
I cut back his ivy. Feet

Deep it was,
And I hacked right

Up to the fence
And woke the moths because

That's where they went
In daytime. Poisonous

Bedrooms unroofed, and the blackbirds
Didn't help, swallowing

Berries whole like fanatics.
And the moths ran still

In their sheets
As if a house

Fire had started at midnight
And snapped shut eyes

In bizarre sunlight, like
Workers on the night shift

Roused by motor bikes. They would
Find other beds, I thought.

II
But later, in that half
Abandoned house, the kitchen

Windows were a museum
Of entomology and I

Became a student of the anatomy
Of moths, able, suddenly, to name

Their parts; costal margin, tornus,
Apex, and I looked

Right into those unfurious,
Beige faces, absorbed

In them, those eyes,
Wide open now

And wanting light but
Not too much. And I

Raised my lips up
To theirs with this

The thinnest slice of glass
Between, and I thought we kissed

Through this, a kiss to get better,
A kiss to remake ruined beds,

As if the moths
Were elderly, or children.

III
But in the rarely used
Spare bed I heard

Their quiet hammering
At my window now,

And I thought of tables turned,
Pestered in the dark by moths

Urgent for ordinary light
As if I was keeper of all

The moons, which, I suppose, I was,
But I'd turned them all off

And still they bruised
Their wings for some answer,

And there must have been
A window open somewhere

Because there was I, naked
And playing blind man's

Buff with moths,
And none of us winning.

IV
In his ward I told
Dad about his ivy.

He was cleaner than
He'd been for years

And imagined the garden
He'd first known and the washed

Toddlers that ran in it.
But did I keep the moths

To myself, when in there
Anyone's life is like wings

On glass, and he needed
To get better, and we all did?

We chose meals and I explained
How hot it was outside.

It was the best summer
Of the Eighties with days

That lasted into the night.
I can't remember.

THE SECRET BATHROOM

I have learnt the names of the rooms,
But what is this one called,
The one whose door is locked?

Like the kitchen it contains water,
I can hear it.
But, I suspect, no knives.

Is it another bedroom?
If so, who sleeps in it?
We are all counted for

In this house
And I would fear a stranger
Plumping up unknown pillows.

If it is a living room
Why is it locked?
To live needs no secrecy,

Just chairs and ornaments.
I cannot remember if this door
Has even been open.

Then the person in there
Must be starving
To death.

It sounds enormous
The way it echoes,
Worse than a church.

Perhaps it is a door
To the outside, upstairs,
Opening to a fall through trees.

But there is a lake in there
And someone swimming
In a hot, flowery summer.

And I notice that all
The walls, ceilings and floors
Of the house are flowing

With rivers as if all
Were melting as an igloo thaws
To a pool of liquid house.

But now I hear this woman's voice
Speaking like a mermaid from the water,
Reminding me how I was once a fish

In her lake, when she,
With her rope of blood,
Angled me out.

HERACLITUS

When he spoke there was
An odour of ignoble gasses.
You thought of striking
A match to bring his speech
To life. He wouldn't
Have minded, being dedicated
To the transgression of all
Fire and safety regulations.
He would have been delighted.
He once increased the voltage
Of his Mum's electric blanket
So that she was sleeping ash
By first light. He lifted
Her dry cinders in his hands
And said that this was the noblest
Roman. He still thinks it.
His sockets are burdened
With clusters of plugs.
He lets his deep fat overheat.
He has no eyebrows. His look
Of sooty surprise is permanent.
One day he will light the blue
Touchpaper and retire. Until then
His Bonfire Night is every night.
And something good, he still
Thinks, will come out of Dresden.

THE SOCIAL INSECTS

Were there ants then
Or just a vision of them

When a Mark Antony
Flexed his thorax to stand

Head and abdomen above
The rest and offered his

And his kind's death
To win them over?

Irresistible incentives.
Sisters lovelier than children.

Cities built on song,
For auld lang syne.

His speech went so home
That when the next age

Of forests came they ate it
And laboured with leaf

Until the leaves dreaded
Autumn, and one insect

In one thousand now
Is an ant. There was dissent.

Caesars rose and turned
To different trees, wanting numbers,

Untempted by a few minutes'
Wings and life in the shade

Of a vast wife. Driven
By a longing for daughters

They evolved through sulks
To some brand new animal.

LANDSCAPE WITH CABBAGES

Mum nurses the good as dead
In the hospital in the cabbage
Fields near the nowhere
To nowhere bridge. Cars rev

In the too narrow lane and queue
To pay their historic toll to the purple
Haired ladies of the bridge which
Isn't paid for yet and tall

Ships don't sail now through
Cabbages by Mum's hospital
Where she tends the accidental
Children with their see through skin

And no muscles or ideas and
Is scared now of the tv's closedown
And won't open doors to unlit rooms
But drives at dawn the round

The houses lanes with bird scarers
And through the one at a time
Bridge beneath the other canal
To find her frosty hospital

And her should never have been
Born children among the soon to be
Harvested cabbage fields
Near the unimportant bridge.

THE EVOLUTION OF FLOWERS

Was it really just a loss
Of composure that caused her

To purchase flowers for her mother's
Third wedding from that aged

Florist at the cemetery gates?
And later, entering Interflora,

Thinking who to send a rose to,
Wondering who would not

Read this gift as a threat,
Thief of air, or prelude

To a blackmail note's clumsy
Mosaic of type.

It was her mistake,
Thinking herself woman,

Thinking herself a rightful
Receiver and sender of blooms,

As if now, reversed, flowers
Searched the bees for scent

She felt violated by blossoms,
Lost in a florist's

That never ended, the world
Just violets for ever

And that the creepy-crawlies
Responsible for roses had left

Their succulent hidey-holes
And come to her as ugly architects

And she wished the world
Rid of insects

And their pearly grubs
Which means a countryside

Of locked up honey and if
That sweet could be released

Elsewise it would ooze
As poison on her toast

And she would sleep
Among the asphodels

Knowing petals finally as fit
Only for potential wives,

Wives and the dead
Who are kept warm

By eiderdowns of bloom,
Pillows of uneaten pollens.

AEOLUS

You do not know you are born.
I have never looked for trouble
But I find it. South of the Horse
Latitudes I am a nothing devil.

On a Saturday of troubled weddings
Brides will blame me if their unions fail.
My ears are wet
With the saliva of cyclists.

At the seasides I made
I have seen whole families
Peg themselves to the world.
I have never jammed a bad face.

This is slander. You do not know
You are born. Let me remind you,
I have conveyed your forests
Nut by nut, brought sugar

To your bitter shores, moved tea
Through narrow straits to where
It has never been tasted. I scold
Rain for raining back in its bed

And send it packing inland.
I have given you a history
Of interesting skies, so when
You next hold out your hand

And an apple lands in it,
Think yourself Newton by all means,
But know why the fruit really fell
And thank me.

THE MICROMURDERS

They had been shadowing her
For months. She felt it

Ever since the time her new
Bag of sugar split and left

A white trail that led to her door.
They followed her from the shopping city

To number one hundred and nine,
She knew.

And the other times
Like when she remembered the clothes,

Patient in their rinse, and postponed
Her Flake to pin them out

On the line, chocolate still
Clinging to her lipstick.

Some spilled onto the grass.
She didn't notice but they did.

They carried it to their nests
As presents for the nursery

Which is like your father coming home from work
With a bar of Mars filling his tipper truck.

She was clumsy only on certain days,
It seemed to go in phases. A month

Of not dropping anything would end
With a crash as a jar of kiwi pickle

Shattered on the stones outside the post office.
She ran before anyone connected the sound with her.

Cats cut their tongues
On the hidden glass in that messy

Breakfast. And there were countless
Other times when she gave herself

Away like that. Carelessness with food
She now saw could cost more than mere

Lack of seasoning,
Want of spice

And the next time she missed
Her egg and the salt crashed

On the floor she did more than just
Toss it backwards. She went

Through the carpet with tweezers
And a microscope finding every last grain

Which was like picking snowdrops in a forest.
It was this microscope that broke

The truth to her. Applied
To herself she saw through its heap

Of lenses that she was lunch
To those things that had found her out,

Hungry things given strange names
By library books, classical mites,

Scholarly ticks, christened in Latin, feeding
On the roots of eyelashes like patrons

Of an exotic delicatessen.
And the Micromurders are now

As she dives into the strongest bath
She can devise, so clean it cleans

The life off her. And what is the dead thing
Now is hard to tell for what

Is the host without its parasite?
What is she without her dirt

But a Christmas dinner gone cold
In the dining-room, the crackers undamaged

And the whole family freezing outside
Watching through glass their meal waste

Its meat its scent its juice its wine
On nothing.

INCHES

Later, we nursed
Our son's sick snowman.

And how he wept when we slipped
Our thermometer into those

Vague lips and saw
His whole face crumble,

Melting to a grimace
That said the pain was only worse.

And those dreams you had
When the snow first came,

Of slide-rules and micrometers,
Of a set-square left in the garden

Whose softly bombarded
Right angle came to nothing,

Must have meant something
About mensuration. Remember

How we taught our son
Three inches, a foot, a yard

By the public standards
Of length at Greenwich,

Pressed home that to ignore
Such sources might

Leave the whole world
Inches out, at least,

Or allow mountains to crumble
Into a cup of tea,

And tea stiffen with fallen mountain,
Like when, that night

Of snowy dreams we tried
To measure our sleep

And found the readings wildly out,
One vast, the other little.

To measure something changes it,
The gauge is a stranger

In an unknown quantity,
Might damage what gain

There's been, which makes snow
Seem the world's real self;

Grainy, vagrant, untrue,
And when next morning our son's

Snowman had turned
To slush, and all his snow

Stolen, our son
Had grown in less

Than a day. Another measurement
We couldn't take.

TOMATOES

Downstairs there was famine.
At breakfast his
Mouth moved on thought-up toast.

His fridge diminished
Its emptiness, full
Of the pretty increments of nothing.

Panic buying had made
The supermarkets just
Broadways of shelves,

And the populace, having
Gnashed through their
Stocks and rations

Could do nothing but
Sit at wastes
Of tablecloth and think

Of planes heavy with bread.
But only yesterday he'd seen
The lorry turning the difficult

Corners, brimming
With tomatoes, leaving its trail
Of fallen wounded.

THE MURDERER IS A COW

He killed in a cow mask.
Discovering tents in the forest at night

He cut through the canvas
Like ripping open a letter

To find the sleepy human
Contents which he knifed.

From her snug sleeping
Bag all the tourist could see

Were the twitching ears of a cow
And a blade as the murderer

Paddled on all fours
On the drenched groundsheet.

And when all the movement had stopped,
Still with his invented face

He blew warm steam from his
Slippery nostrils and licked

With the single muscle of his tongue
The gore.

And then moved off into the forest
Where real cows stepped quietly among

The trees, their careful feet now
And then cracking twigs until his

Shovelling nose came across the green
Membrane of another tent

Where, within, a half asleep hiker
Breathed a sigh of relief

That cows and not killers
Sniffed tents in the forest.

THE STARTER

I was stranded at the beginning
Of everything, up a ladder that had
Been kicked away, but still there,
A bank manager refusing the overdraft,
A station master failing to delay
The train, I brandished my flag
Like one but I was already history
To them, the first page
Of their history, or one drowning
Or waving, or surrendering,

Or Lord Raglan at the lip
Of the valley realizing his error
But denying it. I was seeing
The end of winter, bad weather
Departing, a storm of horses
Taking the first fence, leaping
My own heart and raising turves
On the far side like hats
Thrown at some fiesta.
They'd ruined the spring.

All those small wagers worthless
Like the bulbs that were fooled
Into coming up early only to be
Bitten back by normal frost.
I blamed the grey, buckacting
At the tape, and then I nearly
Throttled a celebrity, but I suffered
On my own private Tyburn from where
I could see the horses, tiny
Now, as if I was six o'clock
And watching the second-hand,
Waiting for its return,
Waiting for the return
Of disappointed thunder.

Aintree's infinity of mud.
It's been heavy going. I watched
The winner who wasn't burn in his steam.
If I wasn't the beginning then this
Was the end. I wake at night,
My quilt a mass of printed hooves,
And sweat in the monstrous silence
That is the absence of horses.

That it should end like this
After such a good start, my life.
Who knows where a circle begins
And ends? At least I can see
The winning-post. The furlongs flash by.

SPEED KINGS

Salt is forever.
The mountains never come nearer.

Two cars, both blue,
Pass from A to B,

Where A is nowhere really
And B only somewhere

That isn't A. Departure
And arrival are hard

To understand, but their
Rate suggests an emergency.

In fact, they passed so fast
You can't be sure

If there were two cars at all,
Or just one that had

Managed to overtake
Itself. And you think

How they, or it, shook Bonneville
Until you thought the lake

Might become a lake.
You wished it would.

GREAT STORM

At the still hub of the machine,
In the panopticon of the storm
He saw three hundred and sixty
Degrees of disaster,

And afterwards everything storm-shaped,
The green belt combed and flattened
To a verdant galaxy, farmsteads
Aligned with grass and trees.

He'd wanted to step out, to be
Blown, perhaps over the rainbow,
But instead registered the perfect
Order of his house, the calmness

Of his cup of tea, the Doric
Straightness of his curtains,
And thought how everything happened
Somewhere else, like the birds,

Still confused and circling,
Wondering what went wrong
With the air, or why
There was nothing left to perch on.

SURVEY

1

As if we'd farmed
Mushrooms in the cellar,
Its walls manifested

An inner self we'd
Dreaded. You dreamt
The night before

Of rot flourishing
Like loaves,
And there it was.

2

The burglars fell asleep
In the cellar, hugely
Lazy on ancient brandy

We'd left there to mature
Indefinitely. Already
It had a wisdom

Beyond its years. Their arms
Were still full of pickings
As after harvest; thirty

Compact discs, the toucans
We made, our leaping
Cats, half burnt candles,

My jacket from Alexander's,
New York, strange things, soap,
A hair drier, stranger

Than the things they left,
Over a thousand books, three novels
On disk weighing about

An ounce and still
Not finished. They dozed,
The pillows and quilts

Of each other. We would
Have gently picked
Our property from their

Lifeless arms, but we
Might have disturbed them,
They looked so pretty

And young. Nine years
They slept there, snoring
Improbably in the foundations

Of the house, masterminding
In their dreams the crime
Of the century.

We wonder when they'll
Wake and notice. We want
Our things, our cellar back.

3
Thirty litres of poison
Were pumped into the walls
Of the cellar. Dry rot,

Said the man from Timber
And Damp, can live
In masonry, dormant,

For up to nine years.
So that was it. Why
The darkness blossomed

Like that, a sort of
Awakening. He showed us
The tell-tale holes

We should have noticed
When we bought the place
Where, perhaps nine

Years ago, more poison
Was pumped in incompetently.
We should have had

A full structural
Survey done, he said,
Eyeing my library

Of brandy,
An inheritance, passed
Down, still growing.

4
So many strangers.
The man from forensic
Who dusted for dabs

And found none, not
Even ours. 'They've been
Unkind to me,' he said

And left, and left
Grey dust everywhere.
The man who replaced

The window whose daughter,
Jess, carefully
Handled the glass,

And the man who installed
The new video, who said
He was known as the draught

Because he could get in
Anywhere. Our paintings,
He said, were like portraits

Of someone's mind. A dream.
His forgotten dream was of
A miraculous invention

That would have made him
A millionaire.
I made a list of what

Was taken, trying to
Recall the value of everything,
Adding a few items

Here and there,
Like my imagined
Collection of rare

Birds' eggs, my Queen
Anne clock. Reading through
The priced inventory

I realised that
Yet again I'd
Written my life story.

5

Of all they took it is
The things they left
That strike me.

This poem, for instance.
Not long ago I dreamt
I would die

While watching television,
Slumped forward in my chair,
The remote control still

Tight in my grip, that
They would have to lever
Out with forks later,

Giving one last gasp
Of infra-red from my
Fingertips. Of all they took

It was the remote control
I was most glad to have back.
It's always the least

Thing that matters.
They surprise you. I hadn't
Thought of it like that.

LIGHTHOUSE

That night the house
Troubled the householder's sleep
And became a kind of Wolf Rock.

What was the loft was
Where the precious light burned,
And the slates of a tough

Roof turned transparent
And prismatic, focusing
That warm, floating lantern's glow.

An ordinary suburbia
Changed to black, frightening sea,
And everything was round;

Rooms, windows, eyes
As he found his stairs
Went down further

Than there were before floors.
His front door seemed
At the base of a well

As he turned the starfish
Handle and stepped
Into the kelp and shells

Of a one-time front garden
And saw the proof, his house
A tower striped like crockery

Occulting its name
Across hostile brine,
Occurring in the Admiralty

Lists of Lights,
Brother to Bishop Rock,
Friend of Eddystone, ancient

As Pharos, he felt proud,
He saw the ships lit up and safe,
He heard the living captains hailing.